Hamburgers

&

A Holy Man

~

Corey L. Kennard

Area 39 Publishing
Detroit, Michigan

Hamburgers & A Holy Man
Copyright © 2017 by Corey L. Kennard

A CLK Group, Inc. Personal Development Book

Editing by Cathryn & Co. – Detroit, MI

ISBN 978-0-9753477-1-3

For author booking information regarding speaking, training, and strategic coaching, please send correspondence to:

Corey L. Kennard
c/o CLK Group, Inc.
P.O. Box 24616
Detroit, Michigan 48224
e-mail: consultclk@gmail.com
website: www.CoreyLKennard.com

Printed In The United States

To my wife, Kristen,
my daughters, Kayla and Kourtney,
and my son, Corey II.

All of you serve as my daily reminder
that I am truly blessed by El Elyon.

To Dana

With Love,

No person can discover *what*
they can become in the future
until they know *who*
they are in the present.

~Corey L. Kennard

Contents

APPENDIX:

Corey L. Kennard

Hamburgers
&
A Holy Man

- CHAPTER 1 -

THE CALL

"Johnson, get in here, now!"

That was the loud cry I heard from Mr. Dobbs. He was my boss and owner of Asaph International, Inc. As I sat in my office, I could not believe the anger in his voice. During all my years of working for him, I had never once heard him raise his voice at anyone. What could possibly be the problem? As Chief Operating Officer (COO) of this major corporation, I commanded respect from everyone. Yet if those who worked for me heard him summon me with an angry tone like that, I could lose their respect and have trouble putting them in their place. Suddenly, I heard a loud knock on my office door followed by a high shrieking voice, "Mr. Johnson, Mr. Dobbs would like to see you NOW, sir!"

It was the voice of Mr. Dobbs' assistant, Nora. At this point I was getting concerned. I began to think about what could have gone wrong in the past 24 hours.

"Are you in there, Mr. Johnson?" asked the voice of Nora again.

"Tell Mr. Dobbs I will be right there!" I replied sternly.

"Okay, but you need to hurry. He doesn't sound very pleased."

"I'm coming Nora, just give me a chance to finish what I am doing," I snapped.

In reality, I needed a few more moments to figure out what could possibly have him so upset. Let's see. Was there an important meeting I missed? No, that could not be it since I'm the one who calls most of the meetings. Plus, we just closed a major deal two weeks ago that's going to bring in millions of dollars over the next two years. So, I knew he couldn't have been upset about that.

Finally, after about ten minutes of contemplation, I got up slowly and walked to Mr. Dobbs' door. As I approached the corner office, I noticed Nora did not look at me. Now this was most unusual. On every occasion that I can remember, she always greeted me with a smile and a kind word when I came into Mr. Dobbs' office. But this time she said nothing. She simply reached for the phone and notified Mr. Dobbs that I was present. Afterwards, she walked over to his door and opened it for me. As I walked past her, she continued to look away and only shook her head as if in disgust. I then heard the door close violently behind me as I entered Mr. Dobbs' office.

"Did you need to see me, sir?" I asked reluctantly.

"Yes, Johnson. Come on in and have a seat," he said as he greeted me with a firm handshake and took a seat behind his beautiful mahogany desk.

"You are probably wondering why I called you in here, aren't you Johnson?"

"Yes, I am," I said with growing concern.

"And you probably are wondering why I sounded so upset."

"Again, I have to answer yes, Mr. Dobbs."

"Well, here it is Johnson. I have been observing your actions for a little while now. You have been a very good asset to our company. As it relates to our overall bottom line, you are very valuable. However, there are some concerns."

"What concerns, Mr. Dobbs?" I anxiously interrupted.

"Let me finish, please, and I promise I will get to my point," he firmly responded.

It was at this juncture in the meeting that I became greatly concerned about what he was going to say. I had an impeccable track record when it came to the completion of business transactions, but I knew my tactics for achieving such success were not always accepted by everyone, including Mr. Dobbs. But in the end, everyone benefited from the results. My job was not to make everyone happy, but to keep everyone working. So, I could not understand why I was sitting in this situation after ten years of creating a massive amount of wealth for our company.

"As I was saying, Johnson, there have been numerous concerns that I have overlooked because of your bottom line performance. Unfortunately, these concerns will continue to mount and eventually affect how we do business in the future if they are not dealt with now."

I could not take it anymore and pleaded with Mr. Dobbs to tell me the specifics.

"Okay Johnson, one of my biggest concerns is how you have treated our staff for the past few years. This used to be a great atmosphere and work environment. I founded this company on the principle of people coming to work with pride and joy, looking forward to what they could do to make a difference in this world. But lately, all I have heard are complaints from a number of our people on how things have changed drastically since you instituted the new company structure that seems to have everyone working in silos. People are no longer feeling joy. They just feel like they have a job."

"But, Mr. Dobbs, isn't it better to have a few disgruntled employees who are offset by a huge bottom line? You did hire me to eventually take your position as the next CEO and raise this company to a higher level, didn't you?"

"You're exactly right, Johnson. I did hire you to raise this company to a higher level, but this company cannot go any higher if its employees feel 'held down' by your leadership. It's like buying the car of your dreams with a tank full of gas and four flat tires. You may be proud of what you have, but it can't take you where you want to go. Our employees are like those flat tires. Unless they are filled with joy and enthusiasm for work, and unless they feel appreciated, you and this company will not go any higher."

As I listened to Mr. Dobbs, I began to realize the point that he was making. Many times, because of the frustrations and stresses in my own life, I took it out on the employees and made them do things that I, myself, was not willing to do. And I could see how some of them would make a complaint or two. However, I still did not understand how this could have gotten Mr. Dobbs so upset.

"I can see what you are saying Mr. Dobbs, and I hope that I can correct what I have done to the individuals that you are speaking about. I will do my best to make this a more pleasant work atmosphere while seeking to maintain our productiveness."

"That's fine, Johnson, but there is one more concern which serves as the major reason why I called you in here."

"What is it, sir?"

"Well, I received a call today from our newest client."

"You mean that major deal we closed with ATX, Inc.?"

"Yes, that client."

"Well, what did they say? Please don't tell me they were not satisfied with the terms of the deal."

"No, Johnson. That's not the case at all. The terms of the agreement are fine. But from what I am being told, you have been hanging around town with the woman from ATX who structured the deal with you."

"I don't see anything wrong with taking my personal time to celebrate such a monumental deal with the person from that company who helped to put everything together."

I was becoming very frustrated at this point, and I began to wonder why this was being brought up. As an unmarried man, I could not see how going out a few times with an unmarried woman, who just so happened to help us land our biggest contract to date, made any difference to Mr. Dobbs.

"Well, with all due respect sir, I would appreciate if my private life was kept separate from this conversation. I am an adult and so is she. Let's not make a big deal out of who I choose to see."

"Well, Johnson, you know it would really not be a big deal if she wasn't the wife of Scott Jenkins, who happens to be the CEO of that company!"

"Wife? Where did you get that from? Besides, they don't even have the same last name!"

"Listen, Johnson, Mr. Jenkins called me personally today and told me the whole story. Apparently, they have had some marital problems and you have gotten yourself caught in the middle of their situation."

I could not believe what I was hearing. How could Donna not mention that she was married? If I had known that she was, we would have kept everything professional and not have gone out at all. Nevertheless, I needed to fix this situation and fix it quickly.

"Mr. Dobbs, I would like to rectify this at once and let Donna know that we need to cut our personal relationship off immediately!"

"Unfortunately, Johnson, that won't be enough. Mr. Jenkins' call to me was either to let you go or relinquish the contract. As you know, this contract will continue to feed the families of our employees for quite some time. So, in an effort to save our biggest contract ever, I will have to comply with the wishes of the client. Just know that this was a very difficult decision to make. But for the sake of the company and our reputation to potential clients, the sacrifice of one will be necessary for the benefit of the masses. I hope that you can understand the position that I am in. You have worked very hard to bring this company to where it is now, and I appreciate everything that you have done. But this is a contract that we cannot afford to lose. Your final check will be mailed to you, and I will ask you to have your office cleared out within the next hour. Thank you for your service, and I hope that everything works out for you."

Now, needless to say, the company and the man that I had worked so hard for over the last ten years of my life had just thrown me out on the street without a chance to clear my name. There I was, a 45-year-old former COO who had felt like the most powerful man on earth just 30 minutes ago. Without a hint of sympathy, Mr. Dobbs picked up his pen and begin to write as though I was not present in the room. Acknowledging the fact that he wanted me to leave, I slowly got up from my seat and walked back to my office for the last time. As I passed by Nora, I heard Mr. Dobbs ask her to get Mr. Jenkins on the phone, obviously to let him know that the deal was done.

The next few weeks of my life were miserable. I tried to reach Donna several times to ask her why she didn't tell me that she was married to one of the most powerful business leaders in the country while she was spending time out on the town with me. She never answered any of my calls or responded to any of my messages. So, I decided to leave her alone and go on with my life.

I searched for work and found out that there were

not any high paying jobs available for an unemployed middle-aged New Jersey businessman who was looking for something comparable to a COO position that paid what I thought I was worth. Needless to say, in the present economy these positions were definitely not growing on trees. Consequently, I decided to take some time to clear my head. I had not had a vacation in years, and this was the perfect time to take one. I needed to get out of the environment that was causing me to feel depressed. Besides, I always wanted to go to France and experience the lively action of the French society. I immediately got on my cell phone and called one of my good friends and business acquaintances in Paris. His name was Daniel, and he had just moved his business over to Paris a couple of years ago. I had no idea why he suddenly got up and moved all the way there. However, he surely would know the best places to stay and the best spots to eat and party. I was ready to experience it all!

- CHAPTER 2 -

GETTING AWAY

The very next morning I found myself at the airport with my ticket in hand, bound for my much-anticipated destination. I had not yet talked with Daniel. He did not answer any of my calls, much like Donna. However, I left him a detailed message about my situation and let him know that I was on my way. If he had time, I wanted him to meet me at the airport when I arrived. Hopefully, he would get the message in time to respond to my request. But even if he didn't, that wouldn't stop me from making my grand entrance into the country. Even though I had just been fired from what I thought was the best job in the world, I felt like my life was making a turn for the best. I had never felt so free and confident before in my life. For the first time in ten years, I felt like I was in control of my destiny.

Now, where this feeling was coming from, I had no idea. All I knew was that in a matter of hours I would be setting foot on foreign soil with a new attitude and nothing to fear. I was ready for whatever was going to come my way.

As I sat in the airport terminal waiting for my boarding call, I noticed an older gentleman who looked to be at least 80 years of age, sitting across the aisle staring at me. As I looked back at him, he did not move his eyes off me. I began to feel a little uncomfortable. So, I nodded at him to acknowledge the fact that I did recognize his stare. However, there was no response from him. As he continued to seemingly look right through me, I then decided to get up and walk around a little, hoping to get his attention off me. I stepped over to the café to grab a small cup of coffee and to my despair, on my way back to my seat, I noticed him staring at me the entire way. I then decided to simply move my seat. I moved to an area facing a completely different direction. Nevertheless, when I looked over my shoulder, I found that the old gentleman's attention never left me. Here I was, Abel Johnson, former big-time COO, at the airport ready to take the most important vacation of my life, and I couldn't get this old gray-bearded man to stop staring at me. I couldn't take it anymore. So, I decided to get up and give this old fella a piece of my mind. But as soon as I got up, I heard the boarding call for my plane. I reached down to grab my carry-on bag and to my surprise, when I again looked across the aisle, the old gentleman was gone. "*Good riddance*," I said to myself and happily boarded my flight. I was the first to be seated in first class. I quickly sat down and closed my eyes. I had no desire to see who was boarding the plane, what my flight attendant looked like or who was sitting next to me. I simply wanted to relax and not be disturbed until the plane wheels hit the pavement of the Paris airport.

For the first time in weeks, things seemed to go the way that I wanted. After what seemed like a lifetime, I was awakened from my deep sleep, when the plane landed on the runway in Paris. I must have been really tired because I did not feel the plane take off or land. Nevertheless, here I was at the Paris airport ready to experience the journey and adventure of a lifetime. I sure hoped that Daniel got my message.

As I arose from my seat and walked into the crowded aisles of the airport, I looked around to see if my friend had made it. After walking a few hundred feet towards the baggage claim area, there was no sign of Daniel. Then, all of a sudden, a young man came running in my direction with a sign that read, "Welcome, Mr. Abel Johnson". I immediately threw my hand in the air to let him know where I was. He came over and gave me the biggest hug in the world.

"Hi, I am Austin, Daniel's son. He couldn't make it but wanted you to have a warm Paris greeting."

All these years, I never knew that Daniel had a son. I guess when all you talk about is business, any details about your personal life seem to always be left out of the equation.

"Hello Austin. It is a pleasure to meet you."

"Well, Mr. Abel, let's get your bags and get over to your hotel. My dad set up everything for you and will meet you later today after his meeting."

"Sounds good, Austin. Let's go."

After we grabbed my bags and headed for the car, to my surprise, I caught a glimpse of a familiar sight. Getting into a cab outside of the terminal doors was the gentleman that annoyed me with his stares back at the airport in New Jersey. As his cab pulled off, he turned and took a quick look at me and slowly looked away. I couldn't believe it. Here I was in one of the most beautiful places in the world, thousands of miles away from home, and all I had on my mind was an old gentleman who liked to stare at me.

"Are you okay, Mr. Abel?" Austin asked as he looked at me with a puzzled face.

I guess my staring at this cab in the middle of the

busy walkway for seemingly no reason at all caught him off guard.

"Oh, I'm sorry Austin," I responded trying to act like nothing was wrong.

"I just thought I saw someone I knew."

"That's all right. That kind of thing happens all the time around here in Paris. Come on, the car is right over here."

As comforting as his words may have sounded, he had no way of knowing how much I was not looking forward to that encounter happening again. When Austin dropped me off at the hotel, I was blown away by its beauty. All the thoughts of my airport encounter were now a thing of the past. The lobby was decorated with some of the most breathtaking paintings I had ever seen. As elegant looking as they were, they had to be originals and probably cost a pretty penny! Speaking of expensive, I knew by the looks of it that this hotel was going to cost me a fortune. But this was my time to enjoy life and experience things I had never experienced before. It was going to be worth every dollar, or should I say "Euro."

When I got to my room, I couldn't believe what I saw. It was as if I had died and gone to hotel heaven! Everything was laid out in its finest form from the bed sheets to the toilet paper in the bathroom. It almost looked like everything was forbidden to touch. But with the amount of money I was going to be paying, I would be sure to leave nothing untouched!

As I sat down to relax for a moment in my mini paradise, I noticed that the message light on the phone was flashing. For a split second, my old friend at the airport crossed my mind and I would not be surprised if somehow, he knew where I was staying. I quickly picked up the phone to hear the message. To my relief, it was Daniel.

"Hello Abel. I hope all is well. By the time you hear this message you would have met my son, Austin, and I hope that he gave you a warm welcome to Paris in my stead. You are probably now experiencing the beauty of the hotel and your room that I selected for you. By the way, don't worry about the hotel expense. I am a good friend of the owner and this is my gift to you. I should be leaving my meeting around 4 p.m. and would love to meet you for dinner. To save time, a cab will be waiting for you around 3:45 p.m. and will take you directly to the restaurant. I'll see you soon, my friend."

I could not believe what I was hearing. Daniel was doing much better than I thought, and I could not wait to see him and talk about his newfound success in Paris. Maybe he even had a job for an old unemployed fella like me. But the most important thing was to catch up with my old friend and discuss life.

As I took a glance at the clock, I saw that it was already 3 p.m. I did not want to be late. So, I quickly got cleaned up and changed as I prepared to venture out into this great city and absorb what I hoped to be a life-changing experience. Just as Daniel said, the cab was there waiting for me at 3:45. I hopped in quickly and anxiously awaited my arrival to my destination. If Daniel's taste in food was half as good as his taste in hotels, I was in for a real treat. Besides, I was starving and could not wait to sink my teeth into some great Paris cuisine. In a matter of minutes, the cab pulled up to what seemed like an ordinary hamburger joint back home. I leaned forward and asked the driver if this was actually the spot where Daniel told him to drop me off, or was he going to run in and pick himself up a burger and fries on the way? The driver didn't bother to dignify my question with an answer and simply said, "This is your stop, Mr. Johnson. Have a great time."

I slowly exited the cab in disappointment. As I walked into the restaurant, the place was almost empty except for a couple of people sitting near the bar area. Suddenly, I heard a loud voice, "Abel, welcome my friend!"

It was Daniel sitting to my left next to a window.

"Daniel, boy am I glad to see you," I said as we walked towards each other. Daniel smiled as he held out his hand and then he surprisingly grabbed me and gave me the biggest hug I've ever experienced.

"Finally, my friend, you get a chance to experience the good life in Paris," Daniel said with his newly acquired French accent as we proceeded to sit down.

"You're right, Daniel, and I must say it has been a very interesting trip thus far. I can also see that things are going really well for you. I can't wait to hear all about your secret to success."

"Hold up Abel. Let's not get too serious. I want you to enjoy yourself and discover some things on your own while you are here. This is not about me. Although I will share with you some keys to my success, you will soon find out that it is not a secret, but it is information that is available to everyone."

"Well, whatever it is I still can't wait to hear it."

"Abel, you can never be too anxious about anything. Like one of my colleagues taught me about the game of golf. The more you tighten up and think about your swing, the less you will achieve the results you want. But when you relax and allow your body to swing through the ball, you'll find yourself shooting lower scores. So it is with information that you desire. If you relax and allow things to come to you, when the student is ready, the teacher will appear."

"Daniel, what's gotten into you? Along with your accent you sound like a completely different person. When I did business with you back in the States, you were just as high strung as me. You never talked about relaxation and allowing things to come to you. As a matter of fact, if you didn't have it, you went out and got it. It was as simple as that."

"You're 100% correct, my friend. And, as you know, I got burned out operating that way. It was because of that way of thinking that I almost lost my family, my career, and even my very life."

"Your life? What do you mean?"

After I asked him, he looked at me with great surprise.

"Nobody told you, did they?"

"Told me what, Daniel?"

"Abel, I let my life and the pressure of work so overwhelm me that I tried to end it all."

"End your life? How could you do that?"

"I recently asked myself that same question. The answer is that I let things happen that were not to my benefit. I began to communicate less and less with those I loved and eventually I felt completely alone and isolated. I thought the only way out was to check out. So, one night at my desk in my plush office, I pulled out a bottle of pain killers and my favorite bottle of whiskey and emptied them both. The cleaning lady found me in time enough to make a 911 call that saved my life."

"I can't believe what I'm hearing, Daniel. You never

struck me as being suicidal. And you never struck me as one who would crack under pressure."

"Abel, most people who end up taking their lives never show signs until it's too late."

"Well, now that that's all over, thank goodness you are alright."

"Yeah, because if I didn't make it, you would be paying for your own tab at the hotel," he shared with a smile.

The tense moment that Daniel had just taken me through was diminished as we both laughed together and our voices echoed throughout the almost empty restaurant.

"As you see, Abel, my old way of thinking and how I handled business almost killed me. So, I had to start all over again by changing my attitude and my environment. And what better place to start over than Paris, one of the most beautiful places on earth."

"Wow, I guess I never knew how serious things were for you when you left New Jersey a couple of years ago."

I was really surprised to hear what Daniel was saying to me, and I thought about my own need to discover what he had now found. My thought was broken by the growl of my stomach, which Daniel heard.

"I'm sorry Abel. With all this talk about my past I see it has caused me to neglect our reason for meeting here in this place, and that is to eat!"

Again, we both sent our laughter resonating throughout the restaurant as we picked up the menus to order. As I glanced through the menu still expecting to see some fancy French cuisine, I noticed that the only food associated with France were French Fries!

"Daniel, I don't mean to sound unappreciative especially with what you have done for me regarding the hotel and the cab ride over here. But I was expecting something a little different than the average hamburger joint back in Jersey."

"Don't worry, my friend, I already knew how you

were going to feel when I picked this place, which I guess can lead to what I call the law of perception."

"The law of perception?"

"Yes, Abel. You see, what life shows you on the outside is not always an adequate definition of what lies underneath. Therefore, what we see should first be experienced before it is judged. Let me give you an example. Remember a few moments ago when I was talking to you about my flirtation with death?"

"Yes."

"Well, you seemed very surprised by my actions. That's because what you saw on my outside did not reflect what was going on in me. You saw a person who looked like he had it all together, but on the inside, I was falling apart."

"Yeah, I guess you're right. But what does that have to do with this place?"

"My friend, you have prejudged the fabulous food that this place has to offer based on the fact that the restaurant is not full, expensive and running over with high-end entrepreneurs looking for attention and not taste."

"All right Daniel, you got me. Since you know what this place has to offer, why don't you order for the both of us and let me pick up the tab."

"Okay, I will order for the both of us, but I can't let you pay for anything while you are here. Abel, I know your situation concerning your job, but that's not why I can't let you pay. You see, it is my firm belief that if you are going to fully receive what this time in Paris could offer, then you cannot be worried about money. I have learned that in order to get the most out of anything, you need to be concerned with as little as possible."

As Daniel motioned for the waiter to come and take our order, I sat in amazement at the change that his near-death experience had on him. And, in some way, I felt that my life was intentionally connected to his tragedy and triumph. Therefore, I had to openly prepare myself for what I was getting ready to encounter.

- CHAPTER 3 -

THE SECRET INGREDIENT

As I bit into the burger that Daniel ordered for me, I had to admit that it was better than any burger I had ever tasted.

"Aha, my friend," Daniel said, "I can see by the expression on your face that you have never in your entire life tasted a burger as good as that one."

"Okay. I must admit that it far exceeds what my expectations were. This must be the best kept secret in Paris!"

"Do you want to know the secret ingredient?"

"I know, I know Daniel. You're going to now tell me that just like the situation with the hotel, you are also friends with the owner of this restaurant, and he told you the secret ingredient over casual conversation and coffee."

"You are very funny, my friend, and half right. Yes,

I am a good friend of the owner, but he did not tell me the secret over conversation and coffee. As a matter of fact, he did not tell me anything. He showed it to me."

"Come on Daniel. He only showed it to you and did not say a word about it?"

"You are absolutely correct, and if you come here enough, he will show it to you also."

"How Daniel?" I said in disbelief. "How does he 'show' his secret ingredient?"

"Abel my friend, the secret ingredient to the taste of his burger is passion."

"Passion? Daniel, what in the world are you talking about?"

"You see, Abel, the great taste in his burger has everything to do with his passion to please his customer. Therefore, each burger is made with such love and care for the customer's well being that it transfers over into a unique and taste-pleasing dining experience. In other words, his love and passion for people mixed with his love for running a restaurant equals a satisfying and delicious burger that is second to none."

"That's it? That's the secret ingredient for his burger?"

"Yes, and it goes far beyond making a burger. You see, passion is the secret ingredient for success in life. If you love what you do, and you connect that love with a sincere and heartfelt love for people, you will be overwhelmingly successful. And please note that you need both a love for what you do, and a love for people. Just having a love for one without the other will lead you down a path of frustration and failure."

"Well, I don't know if I would classify this as success with so few people in the restaurant."

"There you go again, Abel, with your pre-judging. Success is not based on what we see. It is defined by the goals and desires of a person's heart. As it relates to my friend here, his definition of success is not based on a restaurant overflowing with people, but rather on the satisfaction of each person after they have experienced their meal."

"So, you mean to tell me that if he had only one customer today and that person was pleased, then he would consider that to be successful?"

"Yes, Abel, whether it's one or one-thousand. Success is purely based on how each individual person feels after they have dined."

"Wow, Daniel. I guess I never looked at it that way. In my business dealings, it has been all about quantity and not necessarily quality."

"Do you think that way of thinking may have something to do with you being here now?" said Daniel with a big grin on his face.

"Ouch! That was a cheap shot," I responded jokingly. "So, Daniel, give me some more of this passion stuff. I am sure that it has contributed to where you are now, right?"

"Yes, it has Abel, and it is my belief that there are four additional factors that everyone must be passionate about if they want to lead effective lives. These four are; life, belief, family and community."

"Okay, Daniel, I am with you but don't go too fast. I can be a slow learner."

"Don't worry. Once I explain them, they will be easy to remember, I promise. The first factor is life. If you don't love life itself, then nothing good will come to you. You must love getting up each morning with new and great expectations on your mind. A lot of people are just existing and wasting precious time here on this earth by hating what they do and seeing no end to their monotonous living. I bet you can name about 20 people right off the top of your head who are just existing and not living."

"Yes, I can. And to be honest, Daniel, that list would also include me. But please, go on. I am sorry I interrupted you."

"That's okay, Abel. Sometimes when truth hits home, we can't help but to respond. Well, the next factor is belief. Nothing will go your way in life if you don't believe that it will. Everything great starts with the premise of you believing in your mind that it can happen."

"I don't want to interrupt again, Daniel, but I know exactly what you mean. I have heard so many friends talk about great ideas that had great potential, but because they doubted their ability to get it done, it never happened."

"You are right, Abel. I call great ideas, God ideas. That means if God gives you the task, then I have to believe God will equip you with all that you need to complete the task."

"Wow, Daniel, I never heard you speak from a spiritual perspective before. When did you get off into God?"

"Well, Abel, God is my foundation. I learned that fact when I discovered that I could not do anything on my own. So, I guess you can say that when I found my true self, I found God, and that discovery has made all the difference. And that leads me to what I believe is a true gift from God: family. Everyone who is trying to accomplish something in life needs the support of family."

"Well, how does that include me? I'm not like you,

Daniel. I don't have a wife or any children."

"Family is not only defined by having a wife and children, Abel. Family is support. Those who support you and your goals are the ones who care about you. And the ones who care about you are the people that I define as family. So, as you can see, family can include anyone connected to you, who lends you their support. They just have to sincerely care about who you are and where you are going. Passionately seek those people out and love them with all that you have because these are the people you will need when you feel like giving up or when things are not going the way that you think they should. And finally, my friend, the fourth component to passion is the community. Every great visionary should hold as their ultimate goal the ability to serve the greater good of the community and those living in it. Therefore, there must be a passionate love for your community that drives you to make the best decisions for the good of everyone who will directly and indirectly be impacted by what you do."

"You are right, Daniel. That wasn't hard to follow at all. But why is something so simple so hard to take hold of?"

"Because people become comfortable in their everyday routines and don't want to be stretched any further than they would like to go. Passionate people don't have to be motivated or kick-started. They just have to be directed, and then let go. You'll find that most people don't have this quality. Not because they can't, but because they feel that it will cost them too much of their comfort."

"How then can they change, Daniel?"

"You want to know what worked for me?"

"Yes."

"It was prayer. I learned that when I tried to take my life, I had no right to do so. I didn't create my existence. So, I didn't have any right to end my existence. It was then that I realized that God in us desires to connect with God outside of us. If I am created in the image of the One who created the entire universe, then surely I could create a better life for myself by 'plugging in' and gaining strength from The Source of all existence."

"You might be getting a little deep for me with all that God 'in me/outside me' stuff Mr. Preacher man!"

"Abel, I'm not trying to preach to you. I'm only sharing with you the truth that I learned that changed my life. Besides, whether you realize it or not, you do have God in you. When I accepted that realization, I actually began to live and not just exist."

"Well, I really don't know about this prayer thing."

"Have you ever been in trouble before, Abel?"

"Yes, plenty of times."

"Abel, I'm talking about real serious trouble. Not things that were just frustrating or irritating."

"Well, I guess that time when I was driving on an icy road at night. All of a sudden, a truck came out of nowhere around the curve and the driver lost control."

"And what did you say when you saw that truck, Abel?"

"Do you want the clean version or the dirty?"

"Let's be serious for a moment, Abel. What did you say?"

"I said, God please..."

"Aha! You said God, and then you said something like 'please help me!' didn't you?" Daniel said cutting me off.

"And your point?"

"My point is that what you said was a prayer. The God in you naturally called out to the God outside of you because instinctively you knew that there was nothing that you could do to save yourself. We all have in us the inclination to pray. We just need to know how to properly use prayer as an effective tool to receive the authority from God that we need to be successful."

"So, you are saying that I can pray to God and become successful?"

"Well, almost but not quite. Your prayer should be

for guidance and direction, and then based on what you choose between what you think is best and what God knows is best will determine your level of success. So, ultimately after you pray, you must be willing to submit to God's Will for your life and then success will come."

"Okay, I think I got it, Mr. Preacher. What else you got for me?"

"Let's try the word, position."

"Alright. I'm all ears, Daniel."

"Abel, I discovered that many people are operating in positions that they do not understand, appreciate or see the value of, and this is exactly why they are not experiencing successful lives."

As Daniel was talking, I suddenly became distracted by a figure that I saw at a distance outside of the restaurant.

"Abel, what's the matter?"

"I'm sorry, Daniel. There is someone sitting across at the park who looks very familiar. But please go on, I don't want to miss a word you are saying."

"Well, Abel, I think you just made a good point for me to explain what I mean by importance of position. Because you're facing the window, your position allows you to see things that I cannot see because my back is to the window. And the only way to see what you are seeing is to change my position. You see, when I understand my position and what it can and cannot do for me, I can learn what the perspective of others is based on my position relative to theirs. It is from this knowledge that I am able to make a wise decision."

"Again, Wow! That part is almost as incredible as this burger, Daniel."

"It's interesting that you said that because it is based on this principle that the maker of the burger is able to meet the need of your taste buds in an exceedingly satisfying way."

"What do you mean?"

"What I mean is that the owner has looked at serving you not only from the position of what he wants to serve you, but he also has taken your position very seriously and looked at what you as a customer will want."

"So, in essence Daniel, you're saying that this 'principle' of position has been used in determining how well I am enjoying this burger."

"That is exactly what I'm saying, Abel. The way he wants to serve his food may not be the way you as a customer would like it to be served. So, he has spent an enormous amount of time researching to find out what most consistently satisfies the burger-eating experience of his customers."

"And that's the so-called principle of position?"

"Yes, that's exactly what it is!"

"And you know this from your friend, huh?"

"Yes, Abel, the owner of this restaurant informed me of this as well, and I have been able to successfully apply it to my business."

"Well, I tell you what. I sure would like to meet this owner/friend of yours and learn a thing or two from him myself."

"Abel, I'll do you one better than that. I will set up a

meeting with the person that taught him all of his successful principles."

I was totally excited at this point and a bit nervous about meeting the teacher of Daniel's teacher. I could not believe the turnaround in his life, and I was ready to create a little magic of my own.

"Great! When can we make it happen, Daniel?"

"It's already set for tomorrow."

"You had this planned already, didn't you?"

"You can say that, Abel. I wanted to make sure that you have the chance to experience what I have experienced. There is so much more to life than you currently know, and as your friend, I want you to take hold of your destiny as I have taken hold of mine."

"Just tell me where tomorrow, and I will be there."

"You will receive a call at your hotel first thing in the morning giving you the location."

"Alright Daniel, see you later."

- CHAPTER 4 -

A FAMILIAR ENCOUNTER

It made no sense to me to have the best hotel room in town and not be able to sleep. But that's exactly what happened after Daniel revealed to me that I was going to meet his "master" teacher. The clock could not move fast enough for me! After fighting a few short hours of off and on sleep, I finally heard the phone ring at exactly 6:00 a.m.

"Good morning, Daniel. When will the meeting take place and where?"

The voice on the other end remained silent.

"Daniel, why don't you say something?"

"The reason why I did not respond to you is because you called me Daniel. That is not my name," said the voice on the other end in a very stoic way. At first, I thought that Daniel was playing games with me, but after a few more moments of silence, I knew in my heart that there was something very unique about this voice. Feeling somewhat awkward with the silence, I addressed the person on the other end of the phone again.

"Umm, I'm very sorry but may I ask who's calling?" The voice on the other end simply responded, "If anxiety precedes your quest for knowledge, your actions will always be ahead of your thoughts." As I sat there and pondered over what was just said, I had a feeling that such wisdom could only come from the one whom Daniel told me about.

"Abel, I am the one Daniel has referred you to. But, before we meet, you must promise me one thing."

"What's that, sir?"

"You must promise me that you will never rush to judge or hastily conclude anything another day in your life."

I was so overwhelmed by the power of his voice that I could not deny his request.

"You got it. I promise you."

"Good, because the first principle I want to share with you has everything to do with the promise you just made."

"What is this principle, may I ask?"

"I will discuss it as soon as we meet. Right now, if you look outside your window, there is a cab waiting for you. The driver is scheduled to leave in five minutes. You must get in prior to him leaving or our meeting will never take place."

"But I haven't showered or…"

I then heard him hang up the phone. I had no choice. I had to get into that cab. Therefore, I threw on something and rushed downstairs to make sure that my ride toward knowledge did not leave me behind. As I looked at the cab driver, I noticed that it was the same one that took me to meet Daniel.

"I see we meet again, Mr. Cab Driver," I said with sarcasm as he drove off from the hotel. "Where are you taking me this time, to a rib joint?"

As I laughed, I noticed that the expression on the driver's face did not change.

"That was a joke, man. Come on, lighten up a bit."

Oddly enough, he didn't respond or say anything to me during our ten-minute journey. Then, all at once, we came to a squelching halt.

"This is it, sir. Have a nice day."

After regaining my composure and trying to restrain my anger with this poor driver and his lack of a sense of humor, I looked out my window and saw nothing but a bench by the side of the road.

"Is this it? I don't see anybody here."

"This is where I was told to drop you off. Have a nice day, Mr. Abel."

As I exited the cab, I could not believe what was happening. I took a seat on the bench and watched the cabdriver pull off as if he was in some sort of NASCAR event. I then reached for my cell phone to give Daniel a call to see what was going on. As I began to dial his number, I looked up and could not believe my eyes. Sitting directly across the street from me, on a bench, was the man from the airport!

"Hello, Abel. You may be thinking about breaking

your promise you made to me on the phone, but I'm going to help you out by telling you not to question our previous experience at the airport. Please come and sit down." As I approached the bench in a state of shock, I could not refrain from asking him one question.

"Sir, can I ask you one thing?"

"If you must Abel, go ahead."

"Why were you staring at me, and how did you know who I was?"

"It sounded to me like that was two questions. Therefore, I will honor your stated request and answer only one. I personally choose to answer the first question, and because I like you, I will answer the second question later. Abel, I was not staring at you in the airport, simply because I am unable to stare at anyone...I am blind. However, I did sense your presence and felt your every move. The negative energy you gave off made it easy to sense where you were even though I could not see you."

"But...but why me?"

"Sorry, Abel, I have already answered one question. Now we must move on. I said to you on the phone that I would share another important principle with you as soon as we met. So, are you ready?"

"Sure, if it helped Daniel, I look forward to learning from you personally."

"Abel, it is important to never rush to judgment because you will cause yourself to be at a planning deficit."

"A planning deficit? What is that?"

Now he simply went on talking as if I never said a word.

"Abel, the person who hastily judges and formulates quick conclusions will always create an expected end, and will end up basing all his actions on reaching no other end than the one already etched in his mind. The danger is that a wrong conclusion is always generated by wrong actions. And wrong actions stem from wrong planning. Therefore, wrong planning creates wrong actions, which will ultimately lead you to a wrong end.

Likewise, if the end or conclusion is correct, then correct actions will have to stem from correct planning to fulfill that conclusion. However, in both cases, you end up being resistant or closed to any planning that can render a conclusion other than the one you rushed to formulate."

"Wow!" I said to myself after hearing this very philosophical statement. I really tried hard to act like I knew exactly what he was talking about so I fired back as quickly as I could.

"So, what you are saying is if I've concluded the fact that I'm a failure, all of my actions and all of my planning will be guided and motivated by my self-conclusion of being a failure."

"Correct, Abel."

"So, sir, I can then say that I'm at a planning deficit because my plans are solely based on my foregone conclusion that doesn't leave any room or flexibility for change."

"Abel, I could not have said it better myself."

"Alright master teacher, what's next?"

"Calm down, Abel. We still have a ways to go. Besides, it's my time to ask you a question."

"Okay, I'm ready."

"Abel, what do you call this object we are sitting on?"

"That's easy. It's a bench."

"What makes it a bench, Abel?"

"What do you mean?"

"Think about it, Abel. It's a bench because someone chose to call it a bench."

"Is this the same stuff you taught Daniel? Because with all due respect sir, this sounds kind of elementary."

"Au contraire Abel, it's mastering the simple things that give life meaning. Now think about what I just said."

I had no idea where he was going so I just sat there for a few moments and acted like I was thinking.

"Okay I give up, sir. So, what's your point?"

"My point is that you must go beyond what's on the surface to determine the foundation. A bench is simply a chair that seats two or more people. And even though all chairs are designed by their creator with the same purpose, all chairs do not look the same. Why do you think that all chairs do not look the same, Abel?"

"Maybe the designers don't want them to look the same so that they can make as much money off their designs as possible!"

"Good point. But not what I want to hear from you. You see Abel, all chairs have the same essence we as humans have, a destiny. The destiny of a chair is determined by the design and intent of its creator. This, then, determines how its purpose is to be carried out. Therefore, the destiny serves as the optimal place where purpose is to be carried out. When this bench was designed, its purpose was to be able to seat us, but its destiny was to seat us in this beautiful environment here in the park."

"Sir, how does this purpose and destiny stuff relate to me?"

"You, Abel, are presently here in search of your

purpose. God has created you with the intent to use your talents and gifts to serve humanity."

"But I just got fired from a job where my purpose, so I thought, was being fulfilled. So, now what?"

"You're missing, dear son, the fact that even though you thought you were carrying out your purpose, your true purpose can and only will be realized when it is utilized in its optimal environment designated by your Creator. Although this bench could serve its purpose by me sitting on it in an airplane, I would not want to sit on it in an airplane for obvious safety reasons. Therefore, its lack of fulfilling its destiny can nullify the use of its purpose."

"Oh, so now I think I understand. Although I may have been working for Mr. Dobbs, I have to come to grips with the fact that my destiny might not have been fulfilled even though my purpose was being carried out."

"Precisely Abel."

As he made this comment, he stood up and leaned

on his old crooked cane and began to walk away. "Where are you going, sir? Aren't we just getting started?"

He stopped and turned around as if he was looking directly at me and said, "That is exactly why we are stopping. Always remember Abel, a heart that is eager to learn more benefits the most when it thoroughly chews on what has been taught."

As he turned and began to walk away again, the cab pulled up at the point of my drop off as if right on cue. As I got in, the driver took off. But I couldn't help but look back and watch this strange man slowly walk away in the opposite direction soon disappearing among the bushes and the trees in the park. As his last statement ran through my head, I knew that my anxious heart was not going to allow me to cheerfully chew on what I just heard. But nevertheless, I had the rest of the day to digest it.

- CHAPTER 5 -

JUST LIKE RIDING A BIKE

Like the previous morning at 6 a.m. my phone rang and, needless to say, I asked who it was, rather than to assume (like I did before). Unexpectedly, it was the front desk, "Mr. Johnson, we have this envelope for you and were instructed that you are to pick it up right away."

"Okay, I'll be right down," I responded.

An envelope? What was this, another lesson? I hurried down after getting dressed to see what this was all about.

"Here you go, Mr. Johnson," said the clerk at the desk.

"Thanks. By the way, do you know who left this?"

"No, I don't. It was here this morning when I came in, with the instructions to give it to you right away."

"Well, thanks again."

As I walked to a nearby seat in the lobby and sat down, I anxiously read the contents of the envelope: "Good morning, Abel. I hope you're up for a ride. As before, your transportation is right outside. P.S., the combination is 4-Right, 3-Left, 16-Right. See you at the restaurant at 7 o'clock. Signed, N. Mire" When I got up out of my seat and went outside expecting to see my familiar cabdriver and his poor attitude, he was nowhere in sight. But when I saw what I did see, it validated the reason for the combination mentioned in the note. There it was - a brand new bicycle chained to the bike stand. It was the professional type, like the one that Lance Armstrong would use in one of his many Tour de France championship rides. And sure enough, when I entered the combination, the lock opened, and there I was in Paris with a brand-new bicycle in my possession wondering what in the world was supposed to happen now. As soon as this thought entered my mind, I heard the voice of the person who handed me the note. "Mr. Johnson, I almost forgot to tell you. The person who gave you the note also left this other note and it reads,

'The proper communication will create a pathway to get you where you need to be in thirty minutes.'

"Proper communication will create a pathway to get me where I need to be in thirty minutes? Gee, thanks," I replied, very confused.

Now, if I needed to meet Mr. Mire, which I assumed to be the name of my master teacher, at the restaurant, which I assumed to be the place, without any directions, on a bike, in this big city of Paris, in thirty minutes, then this was probably not going to work out the way Mr. Mire expected! It must have been at least 20 years since I attempted to ride a bike, but since I figured that there was a lesson to learn in this, I hopped on and started in the direction that the cab took me when I first met Daniel at the restaurant. Some things looked very familiar while others didn't. Now after riding for about 25 minutes, I officially accepted the fact that I had no idea where I was. Going against the desires of my ego and listening to the agony of my legs, I decided to stop and ask someone where Daniel's favorite restaurant was located. However, in doing this, I had two things going against me: One, I did not know the name of the restaurant, and two, I did not speak a lick of French and no one around me spoke English! This was a mess! I was officially lost and I knew that I was going to be late. Suddenly, to my surprise, my good old taxi driver pulled up and asked me if I needed a lift. With an embarrassed look on my face, I eagerly said, "Yes!" He got out, put my bike in the trunk and we started toward the restaurant. When we pulled up, it was about 7:15 a.m., I was officially 15 minutes late, and no one was in sight.

"Sir, Mr. Mire wants you to go to the back entrance. The restaurant is not open yet," said the cabdriver, as he reluctantly pulled my bike from the trunk.

"Thanks. I guess I'll be seeing you later huh, cabbie?" I asked being concerned about how I was going to get back to the hotel.

"Don't worry Mr. Abel, everything is taken care of."

As I walked around to the back, I began to hear voices and the clanging of dishes. I slowly opened the door.

"Excuse me, I'm looking for Mr. Mire."

"Sure, come on in. He's been waiting for you at the table inside," said one of the gentlemen who never stopped doing whatever he was doing with some dishes. As I walked in the restaurant seating section, all the lights were off, but I managed to see Mr. Mire sitting in the same booth that Daniel and I sat in when I first arrived.

"Ah, Mr. Mire," I said gently, "sorry I'm late but it's been so long since I rode a bike and…"

"Please Abel, no excuses," Mr. Mire said as he cut me off. "I hate excuses. Excuses only serve as meaningless statements of concern when someone intentionally disrespects the time, efforts and instructions of other individuals. That's why I sent the cab to follow you. Please have a seat and I'll explain."

(This felt much like when Mr. Dobbs invited me into his office before he fired me, like a little kid who got in trouble in school with the principal.)

"Abel, when the gentleman gave you the note, did he give you any additional information as well?"

"Yes, he did."

"I'm sure he told you about properly communicating, right?"

"Yes, he did."

"So, before you started pedaling the bike, did you ever ask for instructions or directions?"

"No, I didn't. I thought I could find my own way and..."

"And you got lost, didn't you?" he said, cutting me off again.

"Okay, I can see your point sir, but why set me up to fail?"

"I'm not setting you up to fail. I'm simply revealing to you your leadership flaws. The reason why you didn't ask is because you thought you could find your own way without any help from others. The problem is that you did not determine your path before taking off. In business and in life when you do this, you end up taking others where you ended up – lost. When there is no sense of direction, there is no focus. No focus will lead to frustration and a lot of wasted time, like you experienced a few moments ago. In short Abel, when you aim at nothing, you'll end up hitting just that, every single time."

"So, sir, the cab was there for me only when I admitted I was lost?"

"Exactly. But often there is no cab in the real world. And as you already know from your prior employment experience that…"

"Wait! Wait just a minute, sir! How do you know about my former job?"

"I told you yesterday that I will answer that question later. Remember at the appropriate time all things will be revealed to the one whose question is not yet answered. Since we are about fifteen minutes behind though, I want to quickly share a few more things with you before the restaurant opens.

"Well, if it means exposing more underlying reasons why I lost my job or why I was a poor leader, then I don't know if I'm ready to hear them."

"That's perfect, because the thing I want to share with you is that as an effective leader you must be able to handle what seems to be very pessimistic views from others."

"What do you mean?"

"Abel, you have to learn how to process things. In other words, it's your perception of the pessimism that will make the difference. Look at pessimism simply as criticism, and criticism is defined as the opinionated feedback of how others view you and your actions. What you must do, Abel, is learn who is in control."

"So, are you saying I shouldn't feel mad when I'm criticized?"

"No, that is not what I am saying. Feeling mad can

be a natural reaction. How you respond to feeling mad is what makes the difference. The key is to look at the criticism as information that needs to be processed. When you look at it this way, you will be on your way to neutralizing and even demolishing the intent of your criticizers. Furthermore, the word criticism has a Greek origin which means to discern. Therefore, analyze what is being said by first considering the source. Then assess that person's intention. And finally, analyze the truth of their statements. Never take criticism personally. It was Eleanor Roosevelt who said, 'No one can make you feel inferior without your consent.'"

"Mr. Mire, I can't believe how easy you made handling criticism sound. Just hearing what you just said now allows me to rethink how I should look at Mr. Dobbs and why he fired me."

"Were you angry about it, Abel?"

"Angry? Man, I was angrier than a balloon patch full of porcupines!"

"But how do you feel now?"

"My eyes have been opened to the fact that all things have a reason for taking place. To be honest, I was not happy with my life. And now I believe Mr. Dobbs helped to release me to a new start in life that I was afraid to take on my own. I can say that it was…"

"Divine maybe?" as he cut me off, yet again.

"Yeah, sort of divine, Mr. Mire."

"Abel, let me share this with you. When it comes to significant encounters, nothing is just 'sort of,' either it is or it's not. It's like saying that a woman is 'sort of ' pregnant. That sounds ridiculous. Either she is or she's not. What you experienced was divine and now you have to begin to embrace the significance of it."

"I think this is what Daniel tried to tell me when he had his life-changing experience. This notion of embracing the divine."

"It obviously worked for him and it can also work for you. And the only way to make it work for you Abel, is to change your approach to business and life."

"And how do I do that, sir?" I said with a tone that indicated that I knew another principle was on the way.

"You change your approach by changing your posture."

"Does this have anything to do with all of that bench stuff you talked about yesterday?"

"No Abel. Posture has everything to do with the confidence and boldness that you live life with. For example, when I started this restaurant, I had to believe that I was going to be the best or get out of the business. How you carry yourself will determine the extent of your influence and the scope of your success. For example, if we were going to be the best, we couldn't just think it. We had to live it. Therefore, when a person walked into this restaurant, it had to be immaculate. Our uniforms are cleaned and pressed before each wear. We make sure that we cook with the finest of spices and oils, and we have all of our potatoes shipped directly from Idaho back in the States."

"Hold up, Mr. Mire. All of this sounds a little extreme for a hamburger restaurant."

"It doesn't matter what kind of restaurant you run, whether you sell steak and lobster or pizza, a successful business never cuts corners anywhere. That's our posture. The moment you slack off in your approach to your business is the moment that you no longer care about people."

"People?" I asked. "How do your uniforms and where you get your potatoes from influence people? I'm sure that your customers don't care about that stuff, just as-long-as their food tastes good. Right?"

"Abel, you must realize that no one tastes food, they taste the environment. Lobster at a truck stop doesn't taste the same as lobster in a five-star restaurant. Why? Because people taste the environment. This also works in the reverse. People will pay $7 for a cup of coffee in a specialized café but will not think of paying over $1.25 at a gas station for the same cup. Therefore, the environment not only dictates taste but it also dictates price."

"I guess you're right, Mr. Mire. People are funny like that."

"And Abel, people will always be funny like that! So, you must learn the art of serving people by giving them everything that they could desire from your business. A person who studies and delivers what people want from their business will be a person who will never go out of business."

As I was about to ask him another question, I heard his watch alarm go off.

"Sorry Abel, we have to leave now. My son who took over the restaurant for me must do a final check before we open in a few minutes. Come on, he should be in the kitchen now. I want to introduce you to him and let you hang out with him for a while. I'm going to have to leave you, but I will talk to you soon."

As we slowly walked back towards the kitchen, a figure came bolting out as if the place was on fire.

"Manny, is that you?"

"Hey Dad? I just wanted to make sure that we are all set before we open."

"Well, just slow down one second, son. I have a person with me that I want you to meet."

"Oh, this must be Abel. I've been looking forward to meeting you. Daniel told me I would eventually run into you."

"Manny, he's going to hang out with you. I have to go, but I'll be back later."

"That's great. I bet you're interested to see how things run around here. Well, walk with me back up front, Abel. I still need to check a couple things out before I open the door for our customers."

"Isn't it quite early to open a hamburger restaurant? Who eats burgers this time of day?"

"One thing my dad always taught me was that people will eat what you offer, anytime you offer it. Besides, who said that pancakes could only be eaten for breakfast and burgers only at lunch and dinner? It's all about what people condition themselves to do."

As he stated this, he finished up with his final check and opened the door. As he unlocked the door, a few people were waiting outside to come in. I guess my theory on eating burgers at any time other than breakfast was immediately proven to be obsolete. As Manny cordially greeted the customers, he turned to me and whispered, "Let's go back to the kitchen. I need to let the staff know that we have some valuable customers." When he entered the kitchen, Manny stopped me and asked, "What do you see?"

"I would say a bunch of people working like crazy, but because I feel a principle coming on from you, not unlike your father, I know that it's deeper than that."

"You catch on pretty quick, don't you Abel?" Manny said with a smile.

"You are absolutely right. It is deeper than that. You see Abel, whenever you see a group of people working as hard as they do, they exemplify a staff that understands the whole picture. It is extremely clear to every staff member that they have a direct impact on the satisfaction of our customers both individually and collectively."

"Manny, that's amazing. How in the world were you able to get all of them to understand that?"

"First of all, it wasn't me. It was my father. He taught all of us that if one customer was not satisfied, it was the fault of the entire team. Therefore, each member must do their part to make sure that all of the team looks good and performs well. For example, a great meal prepared by the cook could be ruined by being placed on a dish that was not thoroughly cleaned by the person washing the dishes. And if the dish ever reached the customer, and they discovered the unclean dish, then it didn't matter how much effort went into preparing and serving the meal. The customer would lose faith in the entire team and their ability to prepare and serve food adequately. Their opinion would be eternally etched in their mind without ever taking a bite."

"And that customer would then go out and bad-mouth the restaurant and deter others from eating here because of one dirty dish."

"That's right, Abel. I once heard it said that the most beautiful picture placed in an ugly frame is in danger of never being admired."

"Or Manny, it can be said that the most beautiful burger on a dirty plate is in danger of never being eaten!"

As we both laughed, Manny directed me to his office where we sat down to talk a little more.

"Abel, do you see these awards and letters of accolades that are hanging on the walls of this office?"

As I looked around and gazed at the impressive amount of honors, I simply nodded my head in anticipation of the next nugget of information.

"Well, every person who has ever worked here has received a duplicate of everything you see here."

"You mean, every employee has every award that

you have here?"

"Yes. Whether they were here at the time of us receiving it or not, we make sure that everyone gets what you see here."

"Isn't that kind of overdoing it? And how fair is it to the people who actually earned the award as opposed to the person who came along later?"

"The way you are thinking Abel, and the way we actually think here are totally different and is often the deciding factor as to whether a business thrives or struggles to survive. Our mode of thinking is that since we are a team, and have all bought into the fact that it is fair to share the blame when things go wrong, then it is even more important to share the rewards when things go well. So, when each person is handed a duplicate award of what this business has received, they not only recognize the honor of being acknowledged as a valuable part of a winning team, but they are further motivated to raise their standards in hope of receiving future honors. It is what I heard a gentleman named Mike Murdock say one time about what he called the 'Law of Recognition.' He said, 'Those who go unrecognized in your life will go uncelebrated, and those who go uncelebrated in your life will go unrewarded, and those who go unrewarded in your life will soon leave your life.' I find that to be true not only with business, but with family and friends as well, Abel."

"Manny, it really sounds like you take care of the people who take care of the people."

"That's great Abel!" Manny shouted as he looked for a pen. "I have to write that one down and add it to the collection. Now, let me see. You said, 'take care of the people who take care of the people.' There, I got it!"

"What did I say that was so important, Manny?"

"You just summed up the essential part of any successful business. Leaders must take care of the people who directly serve the customers."

Although I was not trying to convey a profound thought, I tried to act like I really knew what I was talking about.

"I guess the wisdom of everybody here is kind of rubbing off on me, Manny."

"Yes, I think so. There's just one more thing I want to share with you before I go back out and join my team."

"What's that?"

"Abel, when leaders take care of the people that take care of the customers by recognizing, celebrating and rewarding them, a powerful human dynamic takes place."

As I leaned forward in my chair in anticipation of the forthcoming principle, I could tell that Manny was really excited about what he was getting ready to share.

"Abel, the engine that keeps this business running smooth is how our staff has been made to look at their job as not just a job but a personal experience that is lived out in the most excellent and creative ways. My dad always says that we do not have just one owner, but everyone who is a part of our staff is an owner of the business. Human nature indicates that people tend to take better care of something that they own as opposed to something that they view as belonging to someone else. And because everyone feels and acts like an owner, my job as one of the 'legal owners' is one comprised of facilitation and delegation, not ruling. This makes my job easier and the staff happy."

As I reflected on what I had just heard from Manny, I began to see how my interaction with my former employees was nothing close to what Manny was presenting to me. It seemed too good to be true.

"Well Abel, I don't mean to put you out, but I must go out and do my part in making sure that our customers are pleased. I know that Dad said he was coming back later, but you are welcome to hang out in the restaurant until he gets back."

"That will be fine, Manny. Thanks for showing me the things that you have. I know I can become a better leader and person because of it."

"No problem Abel. Enjoy the rest of your time and go out and order whatever you want."

He then looked around at all his staff, smiled and said, "It's on all of us!"

As I walked back into the restaurant, I saw a very pleasant surprise. My good buddy Daniel was at his favorite table getting ready to have a bite to eat with his son, Austin.

"Hey guys, how's it going today?"

"Well, well, well, if it isn't the master student, Abel Johnson," said Daniel with a huge grin on his face.

"Pull up a chair and join us. We were just getting ready to order."

"I don't want to intrude on your time with your son."

"Intrude?" Daniel said with a disturbed voice.

"That's nonsense! Austin and I would be honored if you joined us. We usually have breakfast here at least three times a week to catch up on some things and to do a little bonding."

"Yeah, Dad has always shared some great things with me about life since we started these meetings. I am sure he shared some of his insight with you as well, Mr. Johnson."

"He sure has Austin," I said as I pulled my chair up next to his.

"As a matter of fact, son, Abel here may know a little more than what I've shared with you because he has spent some time with the man who directly, and indirectly taught me."

"You mean Mr. Mire?"

"That's right son."

"Well, if you talked with Mr. Mire, then I'm sure that your time here in Paris has been well spent!"

"To say the least, Austin. But I find it very interesting that this particular thing you're doing together has been something Mr. Mire has not expressed to me yet."

"You mean spending time with family, Abel?" Daniel asked.

"Exactly."

"Well, I am sure he will get around to it. However, if you'll allow me to share with you what my time with Austin has meant, I'm sure it can't hurt."

"Please, go ahead Daniel."

"You know about what I went through a few years ago. One of the main problems was that I had no balance in my life. Everything was work. As time went by, my wife and I became roommates, and my son was just an acquaintance I spent time with every now and then. Without a proper balance between personal time, family life, work life and all-out fun, we would end up having no life at all. So, I make sure that family time and work time never conflict. Therefore, I do not do family business at work nor do I do work business at home. The two must be separate to maintain my sanity. Since I have made this rule for myself, my marriage has been great, and Austin and I have a great father and son covenant relationship."

"What do you mean by covenant?"

"When we make promises, we keep them. That's what I mean by covenant, Abel. For example, if I say to Austin that I'm going to take him fishing on Thursday evening, I don't let anything concerning my work life get in the way of that happening."

As I listened to what Daniel was saying, I could not help but think about what it would have been like to have my "workaholic" father spend quality time with me.

"Austin, you are a fortunate young man to have a father who thinks the way that he does."

"Oh, I know that all too well, Mr. Johnson. To see where he is now and to think that I almost lost him just a short while ago is nothing but an expression of God's grace, and I'm truly thankful."

As I heard these words from an appreciative son, I looked at Daniel who began to smile and stick his chest out with a sense of pride. What he just heard was a heartfelt sentiment that I would have longed to say about my father, and I could not help but wonder if Daniel really knew how fortunate he was.

"Well fellas, I don't know about you but I'm kind of ready to eat," Daniel said, changing the subject probably for my sake.

"I'm really not that hungry now guys," I said. "Why

don't the two of you fulfill your covenant, and I think I'll just go back to the hotel and relax. Manny gave me a lot to think about today after Mr. Mire left, and I just want to take it all in."

"Or in the words of Mr. Mire, 'a heart that is eager to learn more benefits the most when it thoroughly chews on what has been taught,'" Daniel said as he glanced back in forth between his son and me.

"You got it, buddy. Hopefully I'll see the two of you soon," I stated as I began to get up. Both of them got up as well and gave me a hug that I believe served two purposes. The first purpose was genuine appreciation for fellowship, and the second purpose was sympathy for my heart emitting energy that revealed my hurt of not having the joy and love of a father/son covenant that the two of them were experiencing.

As we said our goodbyes, I went out of the dining area and back through the kitchen to the rear exit without speaking to a soul or even thinking about sticking around until Mr. Mire returned. As I looked for my bike, I saw my dear cabdriver friend waiting for me.

"Mr. Abel, I've taken care of your bike. Mr. Mire wants to apologize, but he will not be able to meet with you again for a few days. He had to leave the country on business, and I'm here to take you wherever you want to go."

"You can just take me back to the hotel. I'll be fine, cabbie."

"Okay Mr. Abel, to the hotel it is! But if you change your mind, here is my number."

- CHAPTER 6 -

REVELATION

For the next few days, I told the hotel staff not to disturb me and to hold all calls. I simply wanted to just sleep, eat and think about the things that I learned since being in Paris. I dwelt a lot on my former job and the mistakes that I made as a leader. Hindsight really is 20/20 when you receive knowledge from the likes of Mr. Mire. I was really happy for Daniel but could not help but feel jealous of his new-found life. I sincerely wanted to be a better person and a better leader. I knew in my heart that I could lead a company again and rebuild my life, and I made a promise to myself that my very next opportunity would not be a wasted one. By the third day of my seclusion from the world, I became increasingly claustrophobic and decided that it was time to get out and get some fresh air.

Since I was in Paris, I thought that I should take advantage of my time to do some exploration. I looked for the phone number of my "personal" taxi driver and decided to spend some time out on the town. I remembered that Daniel mentioned the importance of balance between personal time, family, work and fun. Well, here I was - sick of my lonely personal time. I had neither family nor work, so I might as well have some fun! I had my driver take me to several museums and sites that Paris was known for, and I ended my evening by taking in dinner at an exquisite upscale restaurant with the festive atmosphere that only Paris could provide. (No offense to Mr. Mire's restaurant, but I really did not want to see another hamburger for a while.) As I was finishing my meal I could not believe my eyes! It was Donna walking on the sidewalk just outside the restaurant. My first instinct was to immediately run outside and confront her, however, that could possibly cause me to wind up in a Paris jail for what would look like an attempted assault. My initial impulse proved to be totally unnecessary because she was now entering the restaurant! I waited for her to be seated and made a casual non-aggressive stroll towards her table.

"Hello Donna. What a coincidence!"

"Abel, what are you doing here?" she said with great surprise.

"I'm eating like everyone else," responding with a bit of sarcasm in my voice.

"No, I mean in Paris. What are you doing here in Paris?"

"Donna, I should be asking you that question. Nevertheless, I'll answer your question first. Since I lost my job because of you, I decided to get away for a while. A friend of mine lives here, and I decided to visit him and clear my head."

"Abel, I'm really sorry about what happened. I guess I should have informed you that I was still married. We were having some problems and I really needed a friend. When we were working on the deal, I found that you could be a person that I could talk to. After I found out that you had been fired because of me, I felt really bad and could not return any of your calls."

"So, why are you in Paris, Donna?"

"I live here. I was just in the U.S. to close the deal with your former company."

Just when I was about to inquire further, I noticed a surprised look on her face.

"What's wrong Donna?"

"My husband just walked in. He's been out of town for the past few days and it would not be good for you to be here when he comes over."

I then immediately stood up, bade Donna a brief and quiet good-bye and walked away without drawing any suspicion from her husband.

After paying my bill and walking outside, I looked back in and saw what seemed to be a happily married couple preparing to have dinner. Whatever the situation was a short time ago seemed to have subsided along with any chance I had of Donna's future companionship.

On my way back to the hotel, I tried to figure out why things were happening the way they were. From Mr. Mire's teaching, I learned to call nothing a coincidence. Maybe Donna was in my life to purposefully lead me to losing my job. And because of that, I am finding out who I really am and potentially could become. Whatever the reason, I had to now focus on my future. Upon my arrival at the hotel, my favorite and only cab driver in Paris indicated that this would be my last ride with him. He informed me that he now had another assignment that would not allow him to transport me anymore. For a person who seemed to have very little personality, his good-bye was very warm, beautiful, and heartfelt. I bade him a fond farewell and walked into the hotel. As I was walking through the lobby, the familiar voice of my teacher rang in my ear.

"Abel, is that you?"

"Mr. Mire, how did you know it was me?"

"You have a very distinguished walk. It's now a

walk of purpose. I've come to recognize the power of your steps."

"Why are you here tonight, sir?"

"I had my driver drop me off here after we dropped off one of my business partners at a restaurant. We just arrived back in town from a brief business trip. Sorry, I had to leave without notifying you but it was something that I really needed to take care of. My business partner did not adhere to a key business strategy and I wanted to share it with you tonight, if you don't mind."

"Go ahead, Mr. Mire. I could use an encouraging lesson right about now," I said as I sat down to get comfortable.

"Let me first start by saying that whenever you are confronted with making a major decision in your life, always draw on your past experiences to lead you. The story is told of two hunters who were in the woods in Canada hunting elk. At the end of the day, they ended up killing six elk in all. When they approached their pilot, they were told by him that the plane could only carry four of the elk that they killed. The hunters disagreed and informed their pilot that last year they flew six elk on the same type of plane. The pilot reluctantly agreed to fly the six elk and the two hunters. As fate would have it, the plane ended up crashing. When the pilot and two hunters emerged from the wreck, one hunter looked at the other and asked, "Do you know where we are?" The other hunter looked at him and said, "From the looks of things about two miles from where we crashed last year!"

"So, Abel, in business and life your past will always play an important role in the decisions that you make in the present and ultimately will determine your future."

"That's a great story and principle but what does it have to do with your business partner, Mr. Mire?"

"Unfortunately, Abel, my partner failed to learn from his past business decisions and may have cost us a major deal with a new client. When presenting a proposal, there are four rules that we must adhere to for a deal to be successful. I taught my partner that all four rules must be adhered to with no exceptions. Not just two or three, but all four. The first rule Abel, is that you must state the obvious as plainly as possible to get the initial ear of the client. You must see your proposal clearly, show it creatively and say it constantly. This will let those who are interested in your business realize that you are very confident about your proposal and able to convey it in a convincing and understanding way. The second rule is that you must help your potential client to see that they have a problem that needs to be solved, and you will personally be committed to the process of bringing about a solution. Clients do not like hearing from people who only propose solutions without being personally involved in the solution process. The third rule is that you must appeal to their emotions.

"Wait a minute Mr. Mire. I hate to cut you off, but I have made many business deals without ever appealing to anyone's emotions."

"Abel my friend, I have to respectfully disagree with you. No business deal on earth has ever been made without an appeal to one's emotions. Emotions drive every human being and determine what we are willing and not willing to do. When you make a client feel comfortable with your presentation and/or product, you are appealing to their emotions. When you make a client feel like they are moving positively towards a solution or improvement, you are appealing to their emotions. And most of all, when your partnership with your client makes good 'money' sense, you are appealing to their emotions."

"Wow! All my years as a COO and I never looked at the emotional side of all that I was doing. The time here has really opened my eyes to a new way of looking at business and life. I really wish that you would have come along earlier in my life. Maybe I would still be the COO of Asaph International. Oh, I'm sorry Mr. Mire for taking over the conversation! Please tell me about the fourth rule."

Mr. Mire just sat there in silence for a few moments before going on as if he were waiting for another response from me.

"Abel, before I share this last rule with you, I need to answer a question that you asked me during our first session together."

"You mean when I first saw you on the bench in the park?"

"Yes. Do you remember that question you asked me that I said I would answer later?"

"I actually asked you two questions in one, as you put it. I asked you why were you staring at me at the airport and how did you know who I was?"

"Correct. And I believe I answered the first part of that question but did not address the latter. The student that has inspired me to reveal all the principles that I'm sharing with you is Scott Jenkins."

"Scott Jenkins, the one who runs ATX, Inc.?"

"Yes, Abel. ATX is one of my companies, and I put him in charge."

"So, you knew about the deal that I closed with ATX, and that I got fired because of his wife?" I said in an angry tone.

At that point, I was very upset with what I was hearing and stood up and began to pace the floor. "Why didn't you tell me that you knew all of this?" I said in a very stern and disturbed tone.

"If I had shared that with you, I would have never been able to share all the insight to business and life that I gave you because you would not have been able to receive it. Anger is a blocker. It keeps us from recognizing any truth that comes along in its presence. By the way, Jenkins' wife was only an excuse that I needed to get you here."

"What do you mean?"

"My son, when Daniel told me about a friend that he had in the states who would be a good candidate to learn about the life-changing lessons that I shared with him, I used my pending deal with Asaph International and your close involvement with Mrs. Jenkins as vehicles to get you here. I was the one that forced Jenkins to tell your boss, Mr. Dobbs, that the deal would be off if you were not let go. Everything seemed to work perfectly from there."

"But how did you know that I would come to Paris?"

"I didn't, but when destiny is working things out, you must know that it's going to turn out the way God intended. As I heard a wise person say, 'God is always in the mix.'"

"So, what do you want from me since you got me fired?"

"I don't look at it as getting you fired. I simply played a part in releasing you from your caged experience to convince you that, like Daniel, you too can fly. Therefore, I want for you what I want for all human beings, the opportunity for you to realize the significance of your full potential, to fulfill your purpose, and to reach your destiny."

"It sounds like you are trying to close a deal with me by appealing to my emotions."

"You're partly right. I'm sincerely appealing to your

emotions, but the deal cannot be closed until the fourth rule is addressed."

"Oh yeah, I almost forgot. Now that my anger has subsided, you can go on."

"Well Abel, the fourth rule is to close the deal only when you are able to present other resources that support and assure the client that his needs can be met. Unfortunately, after you left, Scott went over all the details with Mr. Dobbs concerning the deal that included all the rules except the last. And because Scott could not provide other resources beyond ATX that would help support the deal, Mr. Dobbs called the whole thing off."

"You mean the deal that I worked so hard to close was lost because of that one rule not being met?"

"No. I'm saying the deal could not exist without all four rules being met. They do not function separately but work together to make things happen."

Amazing! Here I was in a hotel lobby in Paris, in the middle of the night, thousands of miles away from what I called home, listening to a blind "Holy Man" who sells hamburgers, and learning about the things in life that can help me become a better person and a better leader. This indeed was both the strangest and best time of my entire life.

- CHAPTER 7 -

THE FINAL OFFER

"Abel, if you can sit here with me for a few moments longer, I would like to give you the final two principles that I believe will put you in a position to prosper both personally and professionally. I would also like to offer you something that Daniel received from me. That is my full financial support to start any company you would like anywhere in the world, but there is only one thing that you must promise."

I could not believe what I was hearing. This was definitely an offer I could not refuse.

"Okay Mr. Mire, you got a deal. What's the promise?"

"That you will apply and uphold every principle that you have learned and use them daily in your life as you also teach others to do the same."

"You got it!" I exclaimed.

"I also ask that as I share these last two principles with you that you do not at any time interrupt me. When I'm done, I ask that you simply will go back to your room and meditate on all that has been said without saying a word to me. Agreed?"

"Although I do not understand the request, Mr. Mire, I trust your reasoning. Therefore, I agree."

"Good. Now, I would like to share with you the last two principles that are very personal to me. The first is perseverance. It says in the Bible that "He who faints in the day of adversity, his strength is small." I have always taken this Proverb as one of encouragement because my life has been full of times when I felt like I was not going to make it. I remember when I opened my first restaurant. I poured all my life's savings into it. And my wife, although she eventually supported me, was initially against it. I was a couple of months into the business when I had a horrible grease accident while trying to fix the grill that rendered me blind in both eyes. After trying to keep up with the hospital bills and living expenses, we had to close shop. My wife deemed me a failure and left me a very short time later. After some years went by, I dared to try again with failure not being an option. Although I was blind, I got the right people around me who helped me to fulfill my dream of owning my very own restaurant. It was then that I saw the difference between me and others who have dreams. The difference was in my willingness to persevere despite the obstacles that were thrown at me. Most people find themselves never fulfilling their dreams because they don't realize that dreams cost. If you are not willing to pay the price of perseverance, then you are not willing to fulfill your dreams.

My final lesson to you is to always review your performance. This is something I personally do every thirty days. There are seven key questions that I set out to answer.

The first question is, 'Did I accomplish what I set

out to do?' This deals with understanding how clear my goals were, and how realistic were my standards.

The second question is, 'What changes took place in the initial plan along the way?' This question helps me to analyze my adjustments and determine if they are temporary or permanent.

The third question is, 'Could things have been done differently to make the process more efficient?' This question is needed to keep me from being closed-minded and shutting myself off from greater and better ways of reaching my goals.

The fourth question is, 'In what areas did I fail?' What I have learned is that failure is not only necessary, it is valuable. Failure must be used as a tool and reference to understand, not only why you may have failed, but to help you decide whether or not what you failed in was ever worth doing.

Next, the fifth question is, 'Did I learn from my failure?' Many people fail but have not yet learned from their failures because they end up making the same mistakes again. Leadership guru John Maxwell once said, 'If you walk down the street one day and you fall into a hole, then the next day you walk down the same street and fall into the same hole, it's time to walk down another street!'

The sixth question is, 'Did my staff members feel empowered?' The greatest factor that enables you to reach your goals next to self-motivation is the motivation of your team. If people around you are not just as motivated and eager to reach your goal as you are, then you have not done your job to make them feel empowered to do so. Your power will always come from empowering others. And finally, once I have answered all six of these questions, I simply ask myself, 'If I had to do it all over again, would I?' If my answer is yes, then I am a person who is passionate about improving my life and reaching my goals. If no, then I have simply become content with the way things presently are. The caution here is that being content does not always equate to being satisfied."

After about thirty seconds of silence, I knew that I had just heard my last lesson. As Mr. Mire just sat there with no indication that anything else would be said, I kept my promise and stood up, walked over to him, shook his hand and proceeded to my room. After walking a few steps, I felt that I could not keep my promise and just had to ask him one more question. When I turned around, he was gone with no indication that he had ever been there. Just as he appeared when the student was ready, so he disappeared when the student was done. The strange thing was that as I looked closer at where he sat, I saw his crooked cane lying beside his chair with a note that read, "I'll get this back from you at the appropriate time."

I could not believe it. He knew that I would not make it to my room without saying something to him. When I picked up the cane, I suddenly began to feel a little dizzy. I sat down immediately. Before I knew it, I felt really hot and began to perspire uncontrollably. I could hardly breathe and felt so bad that I could not even call out for help. As I looked around, no one was in sight. As I tried to stand up, suddenly everything went dark. After what seemed like an eternity of silence, I heard a familiar voice.

"Mr. Johnson, Mr. Johnson, wake up! Oh my God, somebody help! Mr. Johnson, Mr. Johnson is on his floor! He's not responding! Call 911 now!" It was Nora, Mr. Dobbs' assistant. Although I could not see anything anymore, I began to sense that people were gathering around me, and their voices sounded familiar as well. Voices of people that I used to work with back home at Asaph. But why were they here in Paris now? Suddenly, I heard the sound of equipment as my body was being turned over.

"Let's see if we can get him back," I heard an unfamiliar voice say.

"We'll work on him on the way to the hospital."

I began to feel my body being lifted and then being rolled swiftly away. Strangely, there was a voice that was the most familiar, but one that I did not expect to hear. This voice said, "Hold that elevator! I'm going with you."

"And who are you, sir?" An unfamiliar voice asked.

"I'm Mr. Dobbs, his boss," he said sounding out of breath.

"Can you tell us what happened?"

"All I know is that I called him to my office, and when my assistant went to get him, she said she opened his door after he did not respond and found him on the floor. We then called you."

"Thanks. That kind of lets us know what we are dealing with here."

"What do you think it is?"

"From what we see now, it looks like a heart attack. Has he been under any stress sir?"

"Well, you know, he's been working very hard on a big deal for us. Will he be alright?"

"We don't know sir. We will do our best and see what happens."

"Thanks, I appreciate it. Take care of him. Johnson

is a very valuable leader here at Asaph, and we would hate to lose him."

- NOTES -

A REQUEST FROM COREY

Corey would love to hear how **"Hamburgers & A Holy Man"** had an impact on you and/or your organization. Feel free to share any stories, notes, or experiences that could inspire others by sending Corey an email to: **consultclk@gmail.com.**

You can also send correspondence to:

CLK Group, Inc.

P.O. Box 24616

Detroit, Michigan 48224

To invite Corey to speak at your next conference or in-house workshop/seminar, send us an email to **consultclk@gmail.com** to request booking information, or visit **www.CoreyLKennard.com** to make a formal request.

Follow Corey on Twitter & Instagram:

@IAmPastorCorey

ABOUT OUR COMPANY

<u>CLK GROUP, Inc.</u>
Developing Solutions by Developing People™

STATEMENT OF PURPOSE

CLK Group, Inc. is an organization with an impassioned vision and drive for nurturing (training) and cultivating (refining) in the areas of leadership, organizational/operational design and management, diversity, and team building. We exist to serve and support institutions (businesses, houses of worship, schools, health and community organizations) and individuals using innovative, practical, proven methods tailored to meet the needs and demands of the client.

MISSION STATEMENT

CLK Group, Inc. is devoted to the building and equipping of strong, capable, knowledgeable leaders.   Showing them "*the way in which they must walk and the work they must do"* through training, analysis, facilitation, consultation, and coaching to secure the present and future visionary objectives of the institutions we serve.

All our concepts are customized to meet the needs of each organization, team, and individuals who desire to raise the level of their performance.

We believe in **"Developing Solutions by Developing People™,"** and we hope that we can be of help to you and your organization!

ABOUT THE AUTHOR

Corey L. Kennard, MACM, is a daring and devoted agent of change, serving as a Pastor, Life Coach, Motivational Speaker, and Partner/Board Member for several community organizations in the Metropolitan Detroit area. He personally has over 20 years of experience in business, healthcare & ministry.

He is passionate about creating a culture that enhances the experiences of customers and employees. His passion has specifically impacted the field of healthcare though his work in leading a spiritual care team at one of Detroit's largest hospitals, and as a faculty member of Duke University's Institute on Care at the End of Life (ICEOL) national training program called "APPEAL."

His thought provoking and energizing speaking style has made him a choice of organizations and educational institutions seeking motivational conference speakers, workshop presenters, or inspiring lecturers.

As a writer, Corey is an avid Blogger, and has been published in the New York Times and the Journal of Palliative Medicine. He has written motivational columns for the Detroit News, and authored a previous book entitled, "Goliath Must Fall."

Corey also serves as the Lead Pastor of Amplify Christian Church and shares his life's work with his wife Kristen. They are the proud parents of two beautiful daughters, Kayla Ariana and Kourtney Lael, and his treasured namesake, Corey II.

- NOTES -

Made in the USA
Columbia, SC
23 August 2018